YOU CAN MAKE IT WORK

TIPS TO MAKE YOUR RELATIONSHIP WORK

ANTHONY EKANEM

Made with ❤ on the Notion Press Platform
www.notionpress.com

Contents

Preface

Man and woman were created to be physically attracted to each other, irrespective of their looks, stature, colour, or other qualities that differentiate one person from another. What causes attraction between the opposite sex is in-built into man (man and woman) from creation. This is why couples fall in love with each other and later get married – just as it was intended by God, the Creator.

However, "many couples fall in love, marry, and assume that the job is completed. They believe that everything else will work out automatically." This is far from the truth. A successful relationship does not come by chance. It must be worked for in love by the couples concerned.

"The cure for all the ills and wrongs, the cares, the sorrow and the crimes of humanity, all lies in one word – 'love'. It is the divine vitality that everywhere produces and restores life. To every one of us, it gives the power of working miracles if we will."

According to Nancy Van Pelt, "thousands commit suicide each year, multitude flock to the courts for divorce while many are in mental hospitals, all for the lack of love and human affection".

Dr Smiley Blanton in his book, *Love or Perish*, says "For more than forty years I have sat in my office and listened while people of all ages and classes told me of their hopes and fears.... As I look back over the long, full years, one truth emerges clearly in my mind – the universal need for love .... They cannot survive without love: they must have it or they will perish."

When love fails, relationships fall into ruins and impossible frustrations deluge those involved and those around them. Such emotional pressure may result in juvenile delinquency, adult crime, alcoholism, and various forms of drug addiction.

You need to love your spouse. "It is love that spins the universe, and when we fail to use love properly, all of life suffers." – Dante. The truth is that we all need love in huge quantities. Love is the single most important force contributing to our total well-being. With love in your relationship, you can forge ahead through life's most bitter moments and withstand insults and cruelty.

A word of caution is necessary here. Do not expect unconditional love from your spouse all the time! This is humanly impossible. You must recognize that your spouse demands a certain standard of behaviour from you before he or she will be able to love you more.

Love – the Woman's Perspective

Love is necessary for human survival, and women have great capacities to love and to be loved. A woman's love is seen in the home when she prepares the family meal, when she washes her spouse's and children's clothes, and when she cares for the children in a variety of other ways. A woman's love is expressed when she speaks to or discusses with her husband. When she rises early to prepare the children for school, her love shines through. Her fervent prayers for the man's success speak of her love. Her warm greetings as the husband leaves home in the morning and when she returns home in the evening evidence her great love for the man.

A woman's capacity to love can bring out the very best in a man. Her love can keep a man from a life of crime. Her love can spark hope and renewed trust in a man – making him feel wanted and important. When a man's hopes and dreams are shattered, her love can comfort him. When discouragement sets in and dreams crumble, the woman can help him build new ones.

The world needs the gentle, loving, affectionate touch of a woman, and the love within her merely awaits the right man to tap its fountain of love and affection. Women also have an enormous capacity for love. Not only do they have to share affection, but they also have a large capacity to absorb love in return.

Often when a young man woos a young woman, he persists all day with sweet words and kind deeds. This suddenly stops as soon as the young man has won the young woman over, forgetting the woman's intense need to feel loved daily for the rest of her life.

Because of her capacity for affection, daily expressions of romantic love are vital to a woman's existence. It is the key to her self-worth, her satisfaction with married life, and her sexual responsiveness. By consistently and thoughtfully expressing romantic love, many men could melt even the most frigid woman.

A story was told of a man who provided his wife with all her needs and wants, but the wife was still very miserable. The man did not realise that his wife valued affectionate words from him more than every material thing he had provided. Many men are unaware of a woman's need for romantic love. This is because, for centuries, the focus was on women meeting the sexual needs of their husbands.

But a word of caution for women is necessary here. Some women expect too much attention from their husbands. The mass media have often portrayed a distorted picture of the realities involved in a relationship. Most women expect the things they see on television to happen in their marriage or relationship. They compare their husband to the here seen on the screen. Some women live in a dream world and imagine that one can live on love alone.

While love and romance are sweet and play an important role in a relationship, it may be reasonable to conclude here that love alone is not enough. "A cake made from nothing but sugar would soon dissolve."

Love – the Man's Perspective

Men are loves, but their approach to love differs from that of women. Men are affectionate by nature, and it is a gross misunderstanding to think that men resort to affection only when it involves sex. Although a man's love may not be so directly tied to his emotions as a woman's, it is still very real. He is just more often practical and less romantic in his demonstration of love.

A man shows his love as he juggles the bank account to buy things for the home, the wife, and the children. A man may feel very little emotion in rising very early in the morning and returning very late at night every day, but his main reason for doing so is his love for his family. Men endure this routine for a lifetime and often for a little more than meals and an embrace at the proper time.

No matter how rough the outside of a man may seem, tenderness and love still lurk underneath the surface. A man by nature is kind, affectionate, loving, and sentimental. He has tender ways and can be deeply thoughtful. And he expresses his love for his family in a variety of ways.

Whereas love does not make up a man's entire existence, he cannot live without it. Love motivates a man to work, plan, sacrifice, invest, expand, and pursue. It is for love that he gives up his singleness, accepts full financial responsibility for her and all children born to the union, and gives away his most prized possession – freedom.

There is no limit to the love a woman can receive from a man when she learns to open the door to his heart, for she can provide the right emotional atmosphere for him to freely expose his feelings and dare to share his love.

CHAPTER ONE

Compatibility Issues

One of the main reasons for problems arising within a relationship is the element of incompatibility. Once the initial excitement of the new relationship wears out, the couple soon finds themselves locked in a situation where they share nothing in common. This can be something positive if handled well, but it usually ends up bringing a lot of negativities into the equation and this eventually leads to the breakup of the marriage.

To ensure the relationship has a better chance of survival; both parties should question their roles and perceptions linked to the relationship. You should discuss compatibility, understanding, cooperation, similar hobbies, types of interests, points of disagreement and joy and any other elements that would dictate the kind of participation either party will extend towards the relationship. When it comes to the negative aspect of the relationship, both parties should be acutely aware of how these situations are tackled and the duration the negativity is present until there is some resolution in sight. There will also be a need to examine how these resolutions are sought and incorporated to get the relationship back on track.

These questions are well worth exploring within the beginnings of the relationship as this helps dictate the eventual course the relationship will take. It is also a good way to gauge the potential for pursuing this relationship and what the eventual goals expected are.

For a relationship to work, both parties must be equally committed to the idea of making the relationship work as best as possible. This includes exploring ways to spend time with each other without the need to be forced into doing so.

Trying to spend time together is very important if the couple intends to grow the relationship and keep it happy and healthy for a long time to come. Without the effort to spend quality time together, the couple may find themselves eventually drifting apart and this may even lead to the eventual possibility of separation or divorce. It is especially important to make time for each other, especially if both parties live very active and hectic professional lives. When this happens, it becomes very easy to use work and other distractions as an excuse to not make time for each other. This of course is a very bad habit to have surface during a relationship.

The following are some recommendations on how to create the ideal platform for spending quality time together to keep the relationship current and strong:

- Before the relationship gets to the present stage, both parties will have done things together that were enjoyable enough for them to consider taking the next step in establishing a relationship. Therefore, making the effort to continue to indulge in these same activities will be beneficial to the relationship.

- Finding new things to do together that both parties will enjoy is another good way to create the opportunity to spend some time together as a couple. These new activities should ideally be the kind that both parties will enjoy, however sometimes it may be necessary to indulge in something that only one of the partners enjoys.

When it comes to keeping any relationship alive and exciting, there is usually the need to spice up things occasionally. This can be done using love letters or perhaps going on date nights.

Simple Ways to Show You Care

In the initial stages of the new relationship, the above two activities are very much indulged in and even expected. However, sadly, as the relationship progresses to a more familiar phase, both parties may start taking each other for granted and one of the most popular ways of the perception becoming evident within the relationship is the lack of love letters and date nights.

Most people make the mistake of thinking that such indulgences are no longer needed or necessary, thus falling into the rather boring routine that will eventually lead to the relationship getting into troubled waters. Couples who fail to continue these activities as the relationship progresses risk being taken for granted, and when outside opportunities present themselves, there is always the possibility of being tempted to indulge in these temptations as they will find ways to justify such indulgences.

Therefore, in the quest to not only keep the relationship as exciting as first perceived, the couple should continue the exchange of love letters and date nights to also ensure there are no temptations to seek such activities elsewhere. Being active in the activities will also allow the couple to look forward to these endearing times and ensure both parties are constantly committed to putting their "best foot forward" at all times. This would include both the physical and mental aspects of the relationship.

Keep Yourself in Good Shape

During the dating stages, everyone usually goes the extra mile to appear appealing and at their best. However sadly, this is not so when the couples become comfortable with each other and are already in the relationship for some time. Experts on the subject strongly suggest not letting one's physical appearance be neglected. This is also true when it comes to the mental growth of the individual in a committed relationship.

Show Pride in Yourself

People don't seem to understand the importance of keeping up on both of these fronts. Neither party will be interested in coming home to a relationship where there is no effort put into keeping each other excited and guessing. Boredom will usually be the result of such disinterest, and this will eventually force both parties to seek excitement outside the existing relationship.

There is always the danger of the stay-at-home partner being the one that eventually allows the mental and physical appearance to go downhill. Some people just don't seem to understand the impact made on each other when there is a total lack of interest in the general upkeep, both mentally and physically. This is especially so when there are so many temptations outside the marriage perimeter, this often reminds the straying party of exactly what they are missing out on. This is often also one of the main reasons why there is infidelity and discord within a relationship that has been in existence for quite some time.

Busy schedules and commitments are often the excuses given for the lack of focus on keeping oneself in the best of conditions, both mentally and physically. If both parties don't make a concerted effort to look good for each other, it certainly gives the impression of not valuing the relationship enough.

Put Your Spouse on Top of The List

Making a spouse feel important and loved in a relationship will benefit both parties as the effort made will not go unnoticed for long. Making someone feel important is not only a delightful way of expressing love and respect for the person but is also another way of cherishing the loved one.

Put Them on A Pedestal

Happily married couples will almost always attest to the fact that treating each other with respect and love goes a long way in keeping the relationship strong and being able to stand the test of time. Besides the more obvious reason such as love and respect for the spouse, this treatment will also show the level of value the individual puts on the existence of the spouse within the context of the relationship. It will also be a very natural corresponding action to return from the receiving party, thus making the relationship even stronger and longer lasting.

The more popular way of extending the attitude of putting the spouse foremost in thought and deed would be to always consult the spouse when important decisions are to be made that would affect each other. Others may include finding ways to keep the spouse happy and contented within the relationship, by making a conscious effort to indulge in or arrange for activities that would make the spouse feel special and loved and even buying small gifts for no reason, except to express love. Simple acts that don't cause a lot of work or money such as opening a door or pulling out a chair for the spouse will go a long way in making the spouse feel special and loved. Always choosing to spend quality time with the spouse whenever the opportunity presents itself is also one way of putting the spouse at the top of the list.

A relationship is not something that should be taken lightly, and this is even more so when there are signs within the relationship that signify some level of trouble brewing. Most people try to take the necessary steps to save the relationship before throwing in the towel or raising the white flag in defeat.

Don't Give Up!

Every relationship is worth saving, and it would certainly be worth the effort to try and salvage what was once something beautiful. This is an even more important exercise if there are children involved. The following are some ways to explore if both parties are interested in attempting to save the relationship:

- Set aside some time to talk about things that have caused the relationship to lose its lustre. This may not be easy to do without outside help such as a support group or counselling sessions. Attempting to do so without guidance may cause the couple to get into an argument or worse, into a fighting match where unfounded accusations will make the situation even worse.

- Genuinely seeking another chance to make the relationship work is another option to explore in the quest towards saving the union. Sometimes asking for another chance and then taking all the necessary steps to ensure genuine effort is made will help both parties view the relationship in a different light. Active participation towards the end goal of saving the relationship will require commitment and perseverance.

- Some people may decide to make physical life-changing decisions to prove their sincerity toward wanting to save the relationship. These may include changing jobs, relocating to a quieter neighbourhood to create a better quality of life or even new activities.

There is no point in giving up on marriage and wasting many years and much effort. If there is still love in the picture, there is still a chance of fixing things. However, it is important to know when a relationship is better ended such as a toxic or abusive situation. If there is still a spark there though you should try some of the above tips to fix your marriage, after all some people believe you only get one shot at true love.

CHAPTER TWO

The Right Partner

A good way to picture the basis of a marriage is as a team. Teams usually work well when there are several different factors in place such as cooperation, communication, understanding and other similar characteristics. Being able to have all these good qualities within the marriage relationship will allow both parties to live comfortably and peacefully with each other and this should ideally be the goal to look towards achieving.

However, because of the many challenges in life, it may often be quite difficult to focus on enjoying the marriage relationship without some conscious efforts that will help keep both parties focused on the good elements within the relationship rather than on its negativity. Most experts would attest to the fact that perhaps the most important element that should be prevalent within the marriage relationship should be communication.

Good communication has always been rated as the most important ingredient to cultivate if the marriage is to have a reasonable fighting chance of succeeding. This simple yet very powerful tool allows both parties to be fully aware of each other's thoughts, dreams, perceptions, needs, wants, and a host of other informative bits of information that will allow both to coexist, create and maintain a strong relationship that will last for the long run.

The ability to be emphatic is also another good quality to practise. This element within the "team" will help both parties be more in tune with each other's feelings thus creating a more giving rather than simply taking attitude. Everyone would like to be treated with respect and dignity, and this is even more important as the marriage ages. Most couples tend to make the mistake of taking each other for granted and this is usually the main cause of frustration within the partnership.

Explore Your Values

Every individual should have their value system in place, and this is usually formed as the individual ages from a young adult into a more mature and productive participant in society. Having good values in place will help the person through life's journey and will be a guiding point for most decisions made.

What Is Expected

Being able to explore the values of an individual and as a couple would be something that would be worth doing for many reasons of which compatibility would be the most important one to consider. Having compatible values will not only make the growth of the relationship more positive and workable, but it will also help to keep them committed to the relationship through thick and thin. These values will help to define how both parties within the relationship think, behave, and look upon each other thus making it the driving force behind the relationship.

Some of the core elements that would define an individual's value system would have to include ambition, competency, individuality, equality, service, responsibility, respect, dedication, accountability, empowerment, wisdom, independence, persistence, optimism, flexibility, and a host of other connective mental and physical thought processes.

Most values are made up as the individual goes through various experiences in life or family values being passed on. These values are seen clearly through the way an individual functions in daily life and this is a very good way to gauge a person's suitability as a potential partner within a relationship.

Having good values in place and having values that are compatible or complimenting will help both parties feel more comfortable and relaxed within the relationship. This is especially important when there are major decisions to be made as a couple, where the values would play a pivotal role in the process.

Decide What You Will Not Put Up With

When two people decide to get into a relationship, several adjustments will often be made and most of these adjustments are easy to accommodate and live with.

However, when it comes to making a complete change, this expectancy can be rather unrealistic as some things or habits are not easy to change no matter what the circumstances are. When it comes to elements such as values, it would be very hard indeed to get the person to change overnight or even at all. Initially, it may not be a good idea to impose on the other party all the things that are acceptable and not acceptable for the individual. However, in the long run, this is probably a very good idea as it will save a lot of time and perhaps even some heartache if both parties find that they are unable or unwilling to change certain things about themselves. If this is understood and accepted early on within the new relationship, then both parties will be able to move on to a stronger and more focused level. Therefore, in the interest of keeping sane within a relationship, both parties should be forthcoming with what they are willing to put up with and what they are not willing to compromise on.

This level of honesty will certainly help both parties to understand each other better and to decide if there is any future in pursuing this partnership. It is very important to note, that going into a relationship with the intention of trying to change the other party would be an uphill battle and almost always detrimental to the relationship. Thus, the need to decide and accept or leave the relationship before it gets too difficult to do so.

Develop A Mental Image of Your Ideal Mate

Most people have some idea of what they want their future partner to be like and subconsciously seek such a person out during the dating game.

Not all people succeed in finding the exact match and sometimes tend to settle for the next best available option. However, with a mental image firmly in place, the individual will be able to make a concerted effort in the right direction and will probably be in a better position to make a good pick.

The following are some of the elements that should ideally make up the demeanour of the ideal mate:

Maturity – this is of course a very important element to possess, as mature individuals tend to make more stablemates and are more reliable and experienced in handling the various complications within a relationship. This will further benefit the couples in many ways if the relationship eventually evolves into marriage and having children.

Openness – being open is another good quality to look for in a mate. The ability to be impartial and open about any things will give both parties the option to explore various issues without the threat of getting into an argument or even worse affecting the relationship negatively.

Honestly and integrity – are ideal traits to possess as these too will have a positive impact on the relationship. This is especially useful when faced with painful decisions or situations where honesty and integrity will allow the situation to be resolved in the best possible way while decreasing any impact of negativity with the said decision made.

Affectionate – for some people this is a very natural disposition to have and express, while for others it may be something of a challenge to express themselves or receive affection without being uncomfortable in some way or another.

Meet Like-Minded People

Meeting people is not something that should be taken lightly, especially if the individual is on the lookout for a potential mate or life partner. Doing a little research and making a conscious effort to go out and about will better the chances of being able to meet with new and interesting people and contribute positively to the task of finding a suitable life partner.

One of the best ways of ensuring the task of finding a life partner, who would be deemed suitable, would be to seek out wholesome activities in which like-minded people are likely to be part. This would certainly be beneficial to the eventual relationship as both parties would already have something in common thus paving the way to other connections that could be potentially equally enjoyable. These wholesome activities should ideally be something the individual is fully prepared to indulge in, as this would be a very important factor that dictates the success of any eventual relationship found.

It is important to ensure from the very beginning, the individual is keen and excited to be part of a particular activity and not join simply to snag a future partner. Being fully prepared to participate completely in the wholesome activity will also allow the individual to expand his or her current horizons even if there is no potential mate in sight to be snagged; thus, creating a win-win situation and not an eventual complete waste of time, as this will eventually become very evident to all other participants especially if the lack of interest and enthusiasm is very clear.

Some of these wholesome activities may include more active sports such as surfing, diving, swimming, sailing, kayaking, golf, and team sports or less strenuous activities such as bowling, bridge, mahjong, and many others.

The Importance of Picking the Right Person

A lot of conscious thoughts must be put into the exercise of picking the right person to share a lifetime with. Mistakes can hardly be something either party can afford to make and neither can party flit from one relationship to another until the ideal one is found. This will not only be time and effort-consuming but will also take its toll on the individual living with this kind of mindset.

When couples decide to be part of a committed relationship, there are a lot of mental, physical, and legal issues that would have to be dealt with for them to take the next step in life as one unit rather than two individual existences. These issues can sometimes be very complicated and in some cases require long-term commitments that would be very difficult to evade or get out of.

Making a lifetime commitment to someone is not an easy thing to do and requires a lot of thought and adjustments on both parts. The changes made are significant and if the relationship eventually runs its course or the notion of calling it quits is very evident, then losses will be incurred on both sides which can sometimes be rather hard to recover from.

Both emotionally and financially, both individuals will have to start all over again and this is certainly not a very pleasant experience to face. Therefore, making the right choice from the very beginning will help both parties avoid such negative possibilities eventually.

Most people look forward to being in a relationship that will last for a long time, and to be able to enjoy such a scenario, the choice of a partner would be pivotal towards this desired result.

CHAPTER THREE

Accepting Your Spouse

A great deal of discord arises when one partner sets out trying to change the other, for it is basic to our happiness to feel respected, liked and accepted as we are. We feel uncomfortable when under pressure to change our habits, personality, or preferences. At home especially, we must learn to accept differences, tolerate idiosyncrasies, and respect individuality.

Accepting your spouse means that you view your spouse as a person of worth. It means that you like him or her as he or she is and can respect his or her right to be different from you. It means you allow him or her to possess his or her feelings about matters of importance. It means that you accept his or her attitudes of the moment, no matter how they may differ from yours.

Although it is very rewarding to accept another person the way they are, truth is, it is not easy to do so. Acceptance of others does not come easy because of the common resistance to permitting our spouses, our children, our parents, or our friends to feel differently about issues or problems than we do. This does not mean that one should pretend that his/her spouse is perfect. Acceptance means that you recognize the imperfections but that you are not going to concern yourself with these areas. Instead, you determine to accept your mate as he or she is – faults and all.

An important prerequisite to accepting others is one's ability to accept oneself – just as he is. Self-acceptance enables us to become more aware of others' needs and to feel less of an urge to rush in and fix up other people. We will become more and more content to be ourselves and to let others be themselves.

Factors Affecting Acceptance

Temperament is one of the factors affecting acceptance. Some people have a great capacity for accepting others. They are calm and easy-going by nature. Other people are just not accepting of others. They often find the behaviours of others annoying. They have strong notions about what is "right" or "wrong". We feel uneasy around such people because we do not know whether we measure up to their "standards".

The level of acceptance is also affected by the state of mind. Few things bother us when we feel good. If we are tired, overworked, ill or dissatisfied with the day's achievements, very insignificant things may bother us.

Acceptance between husband and wife can be difficult if one or the other – or both – do not possess a charitable nature. But we should realise that we cannot feel accepting toward our mates all the time. Some behaviours may always remain unacceptable to some, such as drinking, smoking, gambling, laziness, dishonesty, or vulgarity. Real people will have feelings of acceptance and un-acceptance toward their spouse during their married life.

Furthermore, acceptance does not always mean "liking", but we can view the situation without open hostility. In marriage, there are dozens of human differences with which we must learn to live. Whether it is a matter of promptness, religious activities, manner of speech, or personal preference of any kind, through prayer and practice couples can learn to raise their tolerance levels and accept basic differences in their spouse.

Forms of Un-acceptance

The commonest forms of un-acceptance are nagging and criticism. Whether it is open criticism, belittling remarks or subtle suggestions and tiny hints, it all boils down to un-acceptance. Words need not be spoken to convey a message. A disapproving glance or a sigh can convey an un-accepting attitude.

Effects of Nagging/Criticism

1. Nagging and Criticism Increase Problems

Your spouse may become depressed or defensive. He or she may begin to punish you in some ways. A husband may become openly hostile and angry, while the wife may become cool, distant, and withdrawn into periods of silence. They may be little sharing. Husband and wife may live under the same roof, yet seldom speak about anything meaningful. In more serious cases, either spouse may seek acceptance outside the home. Children may also suffer from the tension created at home because of nagging.

2. Nagging kills Love

It is difficult for a man to love a nagging woman. Women, too, feel crushed under a barrage of criticism and fault-finding. They find little enjoyment in doing the housework, caring for the children, or preparing meals for a man who criticises their efforts.

3. Nagging Arouses Defences

Being unaccepted as we are, is a basic human need, and we search until we find it. Unacceptance wounds pride, hurts self-esteem, and arouses sentiment. One's first defence may be a verbal counter-attack, or it might come through being stingy, stubborn, lazy, uncooperative, unloving, silent, withdrawn, or through other acts of hostility.

4. Nagging Does Not Work

A woman confessed to listing all her husband's faults on the back of calendar pages. She admitted to driving both her husband and her son from the home with her constant attacks. Neither of them changed.

Considering the problem created through attempts to change a spouse's behaviour – the tension, the lack of communication, and the effect on the children – is it worth it? Is changing your spouse to suit your ideas more important than a happy home, a loving partner, and emotionally secure children?

How to Point Out Mistakes to Your Spouse (if you must)

No husband or wife should sit idly by while a spouse offends others through actions, words, dress, or body odour. There are times when mistakes should be pointed out, and you may be the only person who cares enough to do this. When this is done properly, your spouse should not resent it. Learn how far you can go with your spouse, where sensitive areas are, and where the difference lies between inciting anger and talking things out.

You may have a legitimate complaint, but your timing may be off. You may wish to wait until the incident has passed, because both parties may be too close to a situation to view it with clarity. By allowing the emotions of the moment to cool, you will gain perspective and wisdom.

Guard your manner and tone of voice. Do not speak to your spouse as a parent punishing a small child for naughty behaviour. Speak as an equal. Your relationship with one another is more important than any relationship you hold with anyone else in the world. The fact is that others are usually more accepting of our spouse's idiosyncrasies than we are. After all, they do not have to live with the fault, and this knowledge should free us from part of our drive to reform our spouse.

Husband and wife should always feel free to discuss whatever disturbs them, but it should not be in the form of a direct attack. The surest way to weaken affection is to tell someone what is wrong with him or her too often. Nothing destroys love more quickly than a running account of faults. To feel loved, we must feel understood, not criticised, or condemned.

How to Change Your Spouse (if you must)

Perhaps you are convinced that you should pursue the route of acceptance having read the above paragraphs. You are ashamed of past attitudes and actions, but you wonder whether your spouse will try to improve if you practise total acceptance. The thought of facing the future in which he makes no effort to improve is almost too much for you.

Dr Murray Bowen, a professor of psychiatry at Georgetown University Medical School in Washington, D. C., and a pioneer in the science of family research, is quoted as saying "The family is a system. Change in one part of the system is always followed by a compensatory change in the other parts." According to him, a problem never belongs to just one person. If a husband is a compulsive worker, perhaps something in his wife invites him to work overtime. If a wife is a lavish spender, maybe something in her husband encourages this extravagance.

The following three statements would help us understand the above statement better.

1) We can change no one by direct action.

2) We can change only ourselves.

3) When we change ourselves, others tend to change in response to us.

Must You Accept Everything?

It is important to stress here that you do not have to accept everything. You don't have to become a doormat at the altar of acceptance. Accepting everything would mean denying the fact that you are a different individual, a person to be respected in your own right, a human being with a will of your own. For example, you need not accept infidelity in your marriage and sexual immoralities.

CHAPTER FOUR

Communication in Relationship

Although it may seem like rather a basic function to exercise, it is often difficult to simply communicate verbally with each other within the marriage perimeter. Most people find that instead of effective communication, they tend to bicker, and this of course is not healthy for the communication exercise nor is it good for the marriage. Learning how to communicate effectively and without any negative connotations or emotions will help to create an ideal platform for both parties to be comfortable in.

The following are some effective ways to adopt or in some cases avoid being able to establish some form of effective communication within the relationship.

1. **Avoid Using the Cold Shoulder or Silent Treatment Tool.**

This almost always never works and certainly does not help the situation at all. There is a need to speak at some point during this situation as most people would attest to the fact that they are sincerely unsure as to why there is a negative situation in the first place. Therefore, by taking the trouble to communicate clearly and effectively, both parties will be privy to the actual cause of the current ugly situation and then will be able to move forward productively and positively.

Learning how to communicate with respect for each other is another very important element to include in the communication exercise. Making unpleasant and degrading remarks will only contribute negatively to an already unpleasant situation.

Therefore, in trying to get the concerns across and understood, there should be some level of dignity and respect present in the choice of words used. Trying to hurt the other party as much as possible may seem satisfactory for the movement but it is rarely a good long-term solution and might even damage the relationship beyond repair.

1. **Take Time to Communicate In Person**

Due to the busy lifestyle of most people, it has become a rather normal practice to communicate within the marriage relationship by means other than actual verbal communication. This is a very dangerous habit to form as eventually both parties will take the time or make the effort to verbally communicate at all, and this certainly spells disaster.

The following are some tips on how to go about ensuring that verbal communication is a vital part of the exchange within the confines of a healthy and happy marriage.

a. Setting aside a specific amount of time to focus on verbal communication is sometimes very necessary for the couple to be able to maintain some level of intimacy through the communication exercise. This time allotted allows both parties to speak their minds and heart and make each other be understood in a non-threatening manner. Doing so in an atmosphere that is both welcoming and comfortable without any distractions would be worth exploring as it will help to keep both parties focused on each other and on what is being said.

b. Preparing oneself to be able to communicate in a non-combative manner is also important. Taking the trouble and effort to be loving and nurturing when communicating will encourage both parties to be more receptive to what is being discussed.

c. Using endearing terms and a lot of encouragement will also help to facilitate a better exchange. Maintaining a friendly and loving verbal exchange will allow for more things to be accomplished. Listening is also part of being immersed in the verbal form of communication.

d. Without the ability to listen, both parties will not be able to understand the communication session, and neither will any positive outcome be achieved. The ability to simply listen will clearly show respect for the other party.

3. **Tune In to Body Language**

It is sometimes necessary to be able to read into the body language of the other party to better understand what is going on and how to best deal with any surfacing situation. Learning how to read the various body language signs will also allow each party to better understand and interpret the partner's wants and needs and work accordingly to accommodate them as far as possible.

The following are some popular body language signs that can be used to tip off the other party as to the current mindset and general disposition of each other.

Eyes clamped shut, and stiffness in the neck and shoulders generally depict an individual who is either upset or not happy with something. These signals can be used to effectively help to defuse any situation before it goes out of hand and to also help to divert the person's attention to something more pleasurable and less upsetting.

This often takes the individual experiencing negativity away from the offending situation and thus encourages a better frame of mind. It should be noted that not all body language signals are negative. When an individual is in a sexy mood some subtle and not-so-subtle body language moves will allow the other party to respond accordingly should they wish to.

This is important to learn as it will help bring the couple closer when such displays of body language attempts are well-read and acted upon. In most cases when the response is favourable, the party using the body language skills to communicate will be so encouraged and happy, that they would likely make it worthwhile and pleasurable for the responding party. This of course will heighten the communication mode to a deeper and more fulfilling experience.

4. Learn To Be a Good Listener

Learning to be a good listener certainly has its advantages and often it allows the individual to seem like a very caring and considerate person. This is worth learning how to achieve as most people appreciate a good listener over a good talker.

5. Hear

Understanding that listening is anything, but a passive activity is a good place to start. Neither is listening expected to be a neutral activity and nothing else. Good listeners can come up with good workable solutions as they can understand and follow the various contributing factors to any situation being discussed.

Developing the skill of being able to listen carefully also allows the individual to "hear" things that are not being verbalized and yet are important enough to need attention. Sometimes these unspoken bits of information can be more informative than what is being said through the conversation, and when these bits of information allow the listener to act in a manner that is both soothing and helpful to the speaker, a huge number of positive effects can be experienced.

Good listeners are usually people who can eventually become wise people. Listening takes a certain level of restraint and thus allows the person to mull over the matter being verbalized before making any judgment calls or giving any response.

By simply listening, the person is allowing the other party to vent everything and anything until fully satisfied. After this happens the person will then be more receptive to any advice or comments made, thus allowing for some type of solution to be made. Two people taking and trying to get their thoughts and views across will not in any way help an already delicate situation.

6. Be Clear About What You Say

Sometimes the wrong words are used or perhaps the wrong tone and this can create a situation that would otherwise not have been forthcoming. Therefore, in the quest to be clear and understood, the onus is on the individual to be as precise as possible with what is being verbalized.

Sometimes it is necessary to be assertive in both manner and choice of words for the individual to be taken seriously. Without being loud or rude, it is possible to ensure whatever is being verbalized is to be taken seriously and not disregarded as unimportant or frivolous.

Being clear in stating one's needs and wants is also something that should be encouraged within a healthy relationship, as this will allow both parties to learn and respect the other's way of thinking and perception of things.

Avoid getting into the habit of depending on people reading between the lines of anticipating one's needs. This will most likely lead to a huge amount of disappointment and eventual annoyance when things don't go accordingly.

Learning not to apologize for certain feelings and thoughts is also something that should be encouraged as those who consistently back down will eventually not be taken seriously at all.

However, when trying to communicate, it would be advisable to keep all emotions in check and to speak clearly and firmly without unnecessary heights of volume included. Respect is very important to acquire when being clear about what is required as those who are unable to win the respect of others will not be taken seriously at all.

Sometimes it is necessary to repeat the request to ensure the items verbalized are properly understood and complied with. This will allow the other party to understand the importance of the matter verbalized and respect its boundaries.

7. Using A Touch While Talking

Most humans need to be touched especially within the perimeters of a healthy and happy relationship. Without the important touching factor constantly being exercised, both parties will eventually feel the missing ingredient, and this could lead to some detrimental results.

Touching and being touched is something every healthy relationship should experience daily and as frequently as possible. The need for touch is very primal and basic, and stroking this desire will leave both parties feeling cherished and fulfilled.

Not all touching should ideally lead to some form of sexual activity, as this is not only pressurizing but also quite unnecessary. The act of touching should primarily be exercised to convey love, intimacy, comfort, happiness, and any other positive connotations which are healthy for relationships.

A loving physical gesture can go a long way, and some say further than the spoken word. A lot of people respond well to physical touch if there is no sexual connotation to it unless the touch was specifically meant to be so.

Most people are simply unaware of the huge effects a simple touch can convey, thus often making the serious mistake of not incorporating the touch action into the everyday lives within a relationship. Most marriages on the verge of collapse will usually concur with the fact that there was almost relatively no touching within the relationship unless sex was the agenda.

This is rather a sad scenario to live with as touching does say a lot about the feelings of love and closeness of the couple within the relationship. Even when having a simple conversation with the other party, some touching could be initiated to help the person *relax* and be more receptive to what is being said.

The Importance of Good Communication

To have a strong and healthy marriage, most people would have to put in the appropriate amount of effort into the building process. This building process is usually an ongoing effort that should not be taken for granted at any given time.

Committing to good communication will also allow the couple to resolve issues before they become out-of-control problems. Good communication skills will allow both parties to put forth their individual views without resorting to underhanded measures such as insults and other negative verbal expressions.

Being able to fine-tune the art of mutually beneficial conversation will certainly help prepare the couple for times when confrontations surface, as the previous ability to converse well will help to keep both focused on resolving the matter most amicably.

Committing to good communication will also help both parties to explore and find suitable solutions as quickly as possible rather than lingering on the problem. In doing so, the problem can be contained and there are fewer chances of it escalating and taking over the lives of both parties.

There are several different reasons for the importance of committing to having a good and sound communication platform within a marriage. This is sometimes the only means of keeping the marriage alive and well, especially if one party is unable for age or medical reasons to indulge in any sexual activity.

Being able to have a good conversation with each other is very refreshing and enlightening. This is even more important as the marriage advances in years and there are no distractions such as children and jobs to occupy their time. In such instances being able to communicate well and on an exciting level will help to keep the marriage in good shape.

CHAPTER FIVE

Intimacy Issues

Understanding the basis of sexual issues must first be properly grasped before any assumptions can be made about its impact on an individual's life. Several different elements eventually affect an individual's sex life in one way or another.

Research has been able to show without a doubt that there is an unprejudiced analysis of the phenomenon of sex that affects an individual in ways that are radically different from other basic instincts such as thirst, hunger, pain, stress and any other feeling a normal human may have.

Commonly viewed as being a mystery and unique, the individual is affected in ways that are often incomprehensible, when the charm of the other sex is seen through bodily sexual desire or sexual lust. This is usually portrayed in the simplest form of the male's attitude towards it, as it is of incomparably greater moral significance than the attitude to the other bodily appetites. Most males almost demand immediate satisfaction in this area whenever and wherever it seems to take control and dominate their thoughts.

Apart from the obvious depths of the connection, the sexual act can bring, the uniqueness of its intimacy is one of the more strongly favoured responses to expect. The intimacy derived from the sex act is mostly what the female counterpart is looking for through the connection. However, with women and men now more commonly looking upon the sexual act as a mere exercise to create a release from the stresses of the real world, even for a few minutes, the intimacy element is no longer sought after in most encounters.

Most participants still seek to have some level of health and safety issues addressed, before indulging in the freedom of the sexual act, as without the proper precautions taken, the act of sexual intercourse can come with a whole other set of problems both mental and physical.

Female Physical Sexual Issues

It is fortunate for women today, that the issues related to physical sexual issues can now be openly discussed and there are several avenues available for women to seek out. This makes the information on female physical sexual issues more accessible and thus creates a better understanding for all parties over these issues.

When it comes to the issue of physical sexuality, women are more vulnerable than men, as there are usually a lot of underlying connective issues that affect a woman in this area rather than a man. Women are usually affected both mentally and physically by all sexual issues. The actual act of sexual intercourse often has a rather significant impact on the woman in general thus creating a need to be more delicate in handling issues connected to the sexual encounter.

A sexual problem can be anything that interferes with a woman's natural satisfaction gained from the sexual encounter which could range from mental to physical; however, in most cases, it is usually noted to be physical.

Ideally, women should be able to enjoy a few different phases of the sexual act before and during the eventual intercourse, and this should include the stages of desire, arousal, orgasm, and resolution. However, most women are unable to focus on these very important phases, which are pivotal to the success of the sexual act, because there are usually other distracting elements present.

The lack of sexual desire or interest in sex is perhaps the most damaging phase to be in. others may include the difficulties in becoming sexually aroused or achieving orgasm which is a very common complaint of most sexually inactive women. Having to endure some level of pain during intercourse is also another reason for the women to be unable to enjoy the sexual encounter.

Male Physical Sexual Issues

Males do sometimes encounter problems that are directly related to physical sexual issues and if left untreated, the individual will not be able to enjoy a healthy and happy sexual life.

For the male, testosterone levels usually dictate the sexual appetite of the individual, and when this is not in favourable balance, the individual will usually encounter phases of either total disinterest in sex or complete inability to perform the sexual act even when initiated.

The lack of certain hormones within the body system can create an imbalance that results in the lack of sexual desire. Medical conditions are another probable contributor to the disinterest or temporary physical sexual issues. Sometimes even the medications prescribed can be a negative contributing factor to this part of the individual's life.

Other concerns that can affect the male's ability to successfully engage in some level of sexual activity could also stem from the inability to control premature ejaculation. This is often quite an embarrassing situation for the male to bear, thus creating the mindset that is weary of engaging in any normal healthy form of sexual activity.

There is also the worry of inhibited or retarded ejaculation to deal with for some males and this is equally damaging to the male ego. This condition also further discourages the male from engaging in normal healthy sexual behaviour.

There are also sometimes other painful consequences to sexual encounters that force the male to avoid any form of sex. These would include retrograde ejaculation where at the point of orgasm; the sperm ejaculated is forced back into the bladder rather than released through the normal channels and out of the penis.

All these contribute to the negative mindset of the male thus directly impacting the physical capabilities of the individual. When this happens the males usually resort to unhealthy ways to release their built-up sex drives or become put off by sex altogether.

Emotional Issues That Impact Sex

Emotional issues do factor very prominently in anyone's life, as one of the reasons for not being actively sexual at certain stages in their life. However, instead of avoiding these emotional phases in the hope that they will eventually improve or blow over, the individual should seek some form of help to successfully overcome this phase and get back to being comfortable with having regular sex.

Sexual difficulties sometimes begin with unpleasant or traumatic encounters at some point in the past in the individual's life. When these encounters are not properly addressed, they could eventually snowball into a situation where the individual is so affected by the past, he or she is unable to function normally or respond normally to a sexual encounter.

Some of the more common contributing factors would include marital or relationship problems, physiological problems within the individual itself, lack of trust for each other within the relationship, and communication problems which could also contribute to the inability of the person to express his or her sexual preference within the sexual act itself or the phase before the actual intercourse takes place, and any previous traumatic experiences that were not properly dealt with.

Other emotional issues that could impact the sex life of an individual would also include the state of the mind of the person which could be in a depressive mode.

When depression set in, the individual would not only be an unlikely candidate for a sexual encounter but could also cause the encounter to take an unpleasant turn which could result in injury to both parties. There is also the possibility of being sexually abused at some stage in life which causes an emotional setback when facing the possibility of a sexual encounter. Unless these emotional issues are addressed and treated accordingly, most individuals will find that they would be unable to enjoy a fulfilling sexual relationship.

When To Seek Professional Help

Sometimes people make the mistake of disregarding the first signs of sexual problems and instead choose to distract themselves in other ways. This can be a rather poor way to handle sexual problems as eventually, the relationship will suffer, and a lot of unwanted pain and negativity will prevail. Therefore, in the interest of keeping a healthy and functioning sexual relationship, all concerned should initiate professional help at the first sign of trouble.

When one party within a relationship becomes unsatisfied or disinterested in any sexual contact, it is time to seek professional help. This is also encouraged if the frequency of the sexual act has become so strained and minimal that some intervention is necessary before the situation becomes accepted as a norm. Most couples make the mistake of putting off sex simply because of their daily life commitments and eventually don't realize that sex is no longer part of their lives. This becomes even more painful when the realization comes in the form of one party straying into the comforts of a stranger's arms to seek and find comfort. When this is allowed to happen, it is often more difficult to revive the relationship to its once glory.

Other more legitimate reasons could force the individual to seek some professional help, and this would include the inability to function normally sexually. At some point in life, most people would encounter this problem and seeking professional help is the best way to overcome this phase in life. Besides the recommendations that are usually prescribed by the professional handling the problem, there could also be a need to have some form of medical aid added to the equation, to help the individual recover adequately to engage in healthy sexual activity sessions again.

The Danger to Your Marriage

Several dangers could be brought on by the total disregard or disinterest in taking issues for granted. The following are just some issues to be wary of, as they are commonly known to be ideal marriage breakers:

1. Neglecting each other is one of the most common by-products of letting issues go untreated. This is a good indication to each other, that there is no longer any

interest in keeping the relationship strong and healthy as not wanting to face issues the relationship depicts.

1. Depriving each other is also another unhealthy way of creating discord within the relationship. When issues are not addressed adequately, the probability of the parties within the relationship feeling that they are being taken for granted would be very high indeed. This will then create the mindset of trying to make the other party "pay" thus encouraging the negative attitude of deprivation.

3. Dishonesty and betrayal are other products of issues surrounding the relationship not being adequately and seriously addressed. When either party feels that their feelings are not being seriously considered, then they would more likely seek comfort with someone else thus jeopardizing the future of the existing relationship. This is often the most common way that most partners use to get attention or to seek solace.

4. Attacking each other within the boundaries of the relationship will eventually cause the relationship to fail. This is usually another method of venting frustration when the basic issues are not being addressed, thus leaving the parties no choice but to vent their frustrations on each other.

Printed by Libri Plureos GmbH in Hamburg,
Germany